Mind Drift

George Genovese

Mind Drift

The spirit of language strives towards objective ends
and to that end do I commend these words to Spirit.

To my mother

Mind Drift
ISBN 978 1 76109 418 7
Copyright © text George Genovese 2022
Cover art: Chris Genovese

First published 2022 by
GINNINDERRA PRESS
PO Box 3461 Port Adelaide 5015
www.ginninderrapress.com.au

Contents

Seafarer	7
Seeker	10
Hypnagogic Vision	11
Afterimage	12
Homeless	13
The Shelter	14
Those Wonderful Ephemera	15
The Hunt	16
Pink Ladies	17
The Elusive	20
Thirst	21
Ocean, Earth and Vision	26
The Ache	27
Nuances	28
Stranded	29
When Gods First Thundered	30
A Writer's Monologue	31
Haunted	33
Community	34
War and Society	35
Vessel	36
The Double Woman	37
Wax Man	38
Mythic Autumn Spectacle	41
Protean Look	42
Born Again	43
The Decision	44
Cycles – a Rondel	45
A Final Valentine	46
Duality	47

Pinning	48
Lullaby	49
Pettiness and the Big News	52
Barren Road	53
Little Green Transgressors	54
Fishbowl	55
Lovebird	57
Mind Drift	58
House Builder	72

Seafarer

He had returned from a distant journey after
what seemed many years.
He was haggard, drawn, dishevelled,
limping through his speech
and stuttering through his telling.
When he spoke he appeared uncertain, hesitant,
his eyes turned to a distance he
was faithfully straining to regather…

We gave him drink and set a blanket
about his body, settled him
before the fire and put him to his ease…
Yet, an aura of strangeness lingered on him
and when he'd calmed and fell into a kind
of stupor, his speech, just as his eyes,
fell here among us from a vast remove.

He told us of seafaring, described to us
the strange intangibles and prodigies
he had seen, such things as made
one doubt one's sanity, such things as all
men wiser than him would call illusory…
And yet, what could be crazier than
to doubt one's own experiences?

Perhaps he was mad, he admitted, but
could not deny the known world
was in fact bounded by a rim to which
he'd ventured. The closer one arrived
to that point, the more one's knowledge faltered,
the more indefinite things became…

Where certainty lost its grip on things
the voice itself, pitched to its farthest reach
was swallowed up by silence, or,
if a faint echo sounded, returned
a hollow, wizened shadow of itself.

He knew why men imagined wonders
when they approached that point;
the mind there baulked, compelled to forge
chimeras and vague monstrosities
if it were to tell itself it still retained
the ability to grip, for, otherwise,
it might descend beyond that rim
into a void from which none could return,
nor even shape the means to speak of it.

He fell to weeping and repeatedly asked himself
how one could live with knowing all
one's seeking, all one's longing, all
one's singing, never reached into the heart of things?
His vessel had not been up to the task
but he would remake it and return.
This time he would not baulk but go
as far perhaps as any could and, if need be,
sail off across the edge of the world.

He muttered something softly to himself
and as hot tears fell on his hands
assumed a look of stern determination.
Someone questioned what he had uttered
and he stopped, reflectively saying,
that this time he would shape his vessel of
the finest air – that it would be at once
so sturdy it could withstand the blast
of any sudden squall or torrent
and yet so supple as to slip
through any obstruction without hindrance;
perhaps even such a vessel might smash
against the rim of the world
and chaos, insanity, annihilation,
prove the outcome of his venture,
but once he had such a vessel, he vowed,
he would once again be ready to embark
upon the only real adventure left to him –
the shimmering limits of language.

Seeker

You wonder why I'm fumbling clumsily
and why, you ask, I roam like someone lost –
I say, 'Because, the darkness spoke to me…'

It's for my vision's dim fragility,
each ghosted moment flown beyond accost,
you wonder why I'm fumbling clumsily.

And yes, there's much allure still yet to be,
but this will pass, annulled, as soon as crossed
'Because,' I say, 'the darkness spoke to me.'

And since for you this seems futility,
a burdened course whose crop outweighs the cost,
you wonder why I'm fumbling clumsily.

But when you censure why I fail to see
and stand like someone numb with bitter frost,
I say, 'Because, the darkness spoke to me.'

Don't doubt my ailment holds the healing key,
an inner light will be my dark's riposte.
You wonder why I'm fumbling clumsily?
'Because,' I say, 'the darkness spoke to me.'

Hypnagogic Vision

I saw him hidden in the greenery,
a spy who eyed me in a curious way;
in verdant glooms, obscuring scenery,
the Devil squatted on the mossy clay.
Despite his horns, his beard, his shaggy hair,
the piercing pupils of his goatish eyes,
he only stared, quite harmlessly from there,
such that I felt no fear in my surprise;
and then each leaf and branch aroused by him
began to swell with such a quickened surge,
that those expanding, green, prodigious limbs
of primal Being's ineluctable urge
compelled me to affirm a vital force
malefic only in its untamed course.

Afterimage

It seemed the world grew overcast,
the light turned dim and fell to dark,
but then I sensed it had not changed
but for my eyes' extinguished sight.

It seemed that sound pitched into black
until no sound could still be heard,
but then I knew no sound had died
but just my ears shut out the world.

It seemed that smell had been dispersed
and fragrance scattered from its place,
I thought the cause a sweeping gust,
but no, my sense of scent had numbed.

It seemed my taste had disappeared
from sweet to bland to neutral-none,
but sweet is sweet and tart remains,
which meant my tongue had lost its sense.

It seemed that things were phantom shades
which yielded me no tactile bounds,
but then I knew things were the same
and it was I who could not touch.

A voice then asked, 'What of the world,
and where is he who was its I,
and who is this, somehow aware,
and slowly gleaning he has died?'

Homeless

Asleep, a curled-up fetus on the path
outside the church, the worldly sum of her
possessions heaped beside a concrete bed,
she lies oblivious to the din of passing feet.
Conspicuously exposed to the elements,
what led her to sleep in such an awkward place?
Was it just for having to collapse, exhausted,
or somewhere she wanted to be for feeling safe?
Does she dream of being invited somewhere warm,
move now in a former life, when she wore
her favourite shoes and clothes to Sunday school,
there told of a mansion of many rooms
for any weary waif or afflicted soul,
and where she knocks and knocks but no one's home?

The Shelter

So take my arms as bracing beams
and make my heart your hearth,
my mouth a box for lettered love,
its smile my front yard's path –

a path that leads to me for I
a door you fragile waif,
and wait ajar for you to draw
inside where you feel safe…

Allow my eyes to be the glass
your image stands in, there,
and these my legs, foundations firm,
supportive everywhere.

Those Wonderful Ephemera

To sink a body heavily in bed
and relish how it sooths your weary weight,
how even all the traffic in your head
begins to float away as cares abate;
those easy moments where your eye alights
on sunshine fallen in a dappled shower
and flickering blooms, on which a gaze delights,
recall the splendour of a fleeting flower;
a home where din and world are left behind
to welcome friends and solitude, alike,
in any case a place to still a mind
or pass a meal with those who share its like;
an easy kiss, caress, an honest smile,
such mundane, modest things make life worthwhile.

The Hunt

Mostly tomorrow is the rule – the end
I chase that swiftly scurries in a dark
and inaccessible hole; today's tasks too

lope fleetly by, lift startled feet in flight
and shirking gait, fleeing fate past facing
the very much and stubborn still to do.

But in aloneness now, my heart still racing,
a chill hand out that hole of no retrieval,
darkly groping, freezes me in fright;

it's you, my death, and there's no game but I,
the time-strapped prey that turns to face your gun –
my unplumbed meaning – levelled in your sight.

Pink Ladies

What ripe pink ladies on the stall
peep firm of form and lately waxed,
all burnished like irradiant jewels
parading there, cosmetically stacked.

No wicked witch's magic spell
could so allure an appetite
as those full rosy orbs, nor tempt
so well an innocent Snow White.

I grope the best my cash can buy
and crop myself a glossy bunch,
then flop my swollen wallet out
before I claim them in my clutch.

Once home I'll fondle one with care
and linger on its scent with savour,
then, making bold, I'll set my mouth
to penetrate its inner flavour –

and ah that press of skin to lips
before I plough its sweetest heart
will vow a virgin juice so chaste
with not the slightest hint of tart.

But when I sink my eager teeth
into its round and ruddy vesture
there is no crisp or natural crunch
but just a hard compacted texture…

And there's no pure and virgin juice
but just a soulless taste, quite bland,
whose baiting vow leaves me unmoved
like some distasteful one night stand.

I set it down in my disgust
of what mere surface falsely tenders,
a neatly trimmed and outward guile
whose beauty's that of 'pure' pretenders.

Already, where the pulp's exposed,
it starts to turn a rusty hue,
as will the other untried frauds
in just a single day or two.

Released from their deep-frozen state,
exposed, like phantoms to the light,
their out-of-season juvenescence
begins to age before my sight.

From mottling spots to full-blown rot,
they're like a tired trope – clichéd:
the nymph who withers to a hag,
like Haggard's She who must be obeyed!

Of no real substance, depth or soul,
they render to a putrid fluxion,
their hollow forms, imploding, leave
a wrinkled pulp of foul corruption.

Let nature take these wizened crones –
go human meddling to the worms! –
that from the compost they're fit for
she'll make of them regenerate forms.

The Elusive

Her motion enters as a foggy blur
as though I saw her through a drizzled pane,
and she, diffusive, on a background wash
of vegetable green, one fleeting moment there,
eludes the liquid window's picture frame.
Appearance vanishes to a visual hush
while rhythm still mnemonically hums
the tinctured echoes of a tonal train
and feeling crinkles with the crooked rush
of trickling droplets on a spectral plane…
She will return as she has always done
though shaped of other shades, and other names.

Thirst

I walk with dark monstrosities inside
my head, see corpses sit to table to
devour their daily fare. I walk and hear
the din of mingled tears and laughter rise
and sicken to the smell of blood that soaks

my bread. Throughout the clamour of my days,
the chill dominion of my walking sleep,
the turning world appeared as if it were
a killing machine or unappeasable beast
engorging on its carcass of ideals.

Here in a slaughterhouse of raging dreams
and through the crumbling architecture of
derelict thought, where shattered reason moulders
and passion strews its rubble on the floors,
I have, with vagrant fits of clarity

amid my madman's rave, believed and sought
the simple truth of sky, its alphabet
of clouds and age-old promise to an eye
of something one might hope to seize and hold,
as if it taught the grammar of God's mind.

And so in earth and sea, in animals
and trees, I've quested all hermetic sense,
sought out and toiled and journeyed far to come
again to these mnemonic shacks where hope
hangs butchered on meat-racks of rust, come where

nostalgia crumbles with the peeling paint
and earnest longing meets the chilling clasp.
For hand in hand with these three shades: Disease
and Age and Death have I returned to this
parched land; with them, once more, this graveyard gang

and all their retinue, the plagues of man,
not least of which is man's own willing hand,
I've come to my own head's dead end… No use,
I've tried to weave a way through each abyss
that lay a snare for careless feet, have tried

befriending darkness where I fell, intent
on resurrecting a triumphant self,
have lived each labyrinth and cul-de-sac,
endured each maelstrom of each hour's attack
and leaned on paradox for a walking stick.

I have when all else failed, so even said,
'Well, if I must be stripped of everything,
condemned to ignorance or self-deceit,
then I will wed this world of cruel confusion
and lovingly lay with her in her black lair.

And I will sing of her and call her Beauty
that art may salvage something of the sacred,
accept my days retain a primal darkness,
curve and spiral from an ultimate silence
I cannot hope to fathom or command.'

And so I've sought to still my heart, allay
and comfort fear with baubles of distraction,
speak a tongue of kaleidoscopic light and woo
a restive mind with phantoms of perfection.
But even this fair maid remained unsettled,

for I've seen Beauty lift her vestal skirt
to yield the secret of her subtle sex,
seen smiling lips of rosy invitation
agape and groaning like an open grave.
Yes there, beneath that sweet facade, I met

the native face of my transfigured lust,
each beckon gilded with a poison barb
that lacerated my desirous hand,
each soft cajoling deftly confected with
a baited kiss… To love illusion from

afar, allow there maybe something still
retrievable beyond oneself which one
as yet has still not grasped but which in time
might come to hand has some consoling charm,
but to discover that such dreams remain

the stubborn self-perpetuation of
one's own dissembling heart must still offend
the memory of truth that haunts a man.
'At least, there's some small gain in giving up
a lie!' So says my mocking truth, if such

exists. And so I goad myself, 'Move on
with stern defiance, even as you cry,
and let these feet imbibe their miles of dust,
endure the heat and pounding sun, and pine
for succour through these parching wastes of thirst;

stoop as a ragged shadow in the haze
and waver in the distance like a mirage,
as empty, insubstantial as these tracts
of sand, watch visions, dreams, all vanish with
a melting mind. Go on, but just go on,

to where it does not matter, every place
the outcome is the same. Traversing through
this wilderness or prostrate here – your task
and only goal's to wait, to watch and wait
and just endure for something you no longer

remember how to say or even name.
And could you still recall that fugitive sense
that shadows you amid your desolation,
you could not force it to a sound for thirst.'
Once more, amid a pause, the earth beneath

my feet begins to quake, once more I feel
the subterranean convulsions of
compacted darkness germinate and stir.
Above this wasteland of disfigured soul,
incarnadine and incandescent sand,

where shimmering horizons plunge and blur
in sheer abysmal voids, some phasm lifts
itself into the arid air, some dream
that crackles with a sere dry-throated thunder.
Now there, amid the distant haze, aglow

and risen as a beauteous epiphany,
a vision of magnificence outspreads
across those cobalt depths. As if of fine
diaphanous veils or airy gauze that decks
some other-worldly apparition, sheets

of wind-whirled rain descend, undulant folds
unfurled in rhythmic tempo to the tread
of some rare creature's gait. And that soft rush
of sound I hear, a brushing rustle of
her skirt, the trailing music in her wake…?

But no, it's just the sky dry-retching for
relief, the vast and empty sky…no rain…
That almost syllabic limpidity of sound
and liquescent song no more than hissing wind.
Again the desiccated soul remakes

its mask, and throwing up a spectre for
the slaking of its thirst, I see in my
delirium this vision of redemption rise;
there, hovering, I half believe and grasp,
then struggle to give up a new mirage.

Ocean, Earth and Vision

The dreamers stand alone – autonomous,
imaginary sovereigns of their demesnes,
but only earth, surpassing all belief,
can mother their elusive empyreans;
their senses filled by nothing but its surge
throughout the hollows of their blurring selves,
it is the earth they breathe, its voices stirred,
its selfless yielded flesh on which they feed.
A microscopic creature in a drop
of water surely knows its world and way
to be, and gleans itself as other than
its food or prey, while, in its fluid globe
and local reign, will never know its world
contained within a vaster ocean's play.

The Ache

Many have been the bearers of kisses,
of kindness, caresses,
tenderest love –
many have borne me many such treasures
but only one ever an ache for my trove.

Many a hand has mounted my shoulder
in mentoring friendship,
guidance and trust,
bearing for me these priceless essentials
but only one left me an ache when she passed.

Many a time I have thought if this wonder
were phantom or fiction,
or ruse of desire,
a phasmal encounter whose mannerly greetings
could only bequeath me an ache for a prize…

Often in hours of somber reflection
I've sternly resolved
to steel my reserve,
and heaping my riches, lovers and blessings,
so smother this ache with their tangible worth.

Often though, still, one secretly opens
the trove of my treasure
with conquering stealth,
for while many still bear me limitless splendours,
one splendour then stows an ache in my chest.

Nuances

Instinctive gestures are a salient thing
that tell us more than our well-chosen words,
for, unlike words, the verity they bring
discloses what our art would leave unheard.
Your furtive shift of eyes, turned lowly now,
which took in stealth their object of allure,
retreat from me beneath a downcast brow
as they reformulate a look, demure;
and while politeness keeps my ear in view
as do those charming, though distracted, smiles,
which, straining for a loyalty felt due
to me, dissemble but no way beguile,
I know, despite your words and yielded hand,
your heart is elsewhere, dear, than where I stand.

Stranded

By what dispassion my eyes see I do not know –
but here among my things (such things delighted in)
it seems as if a tidal light had ebbed the world
to leave some creature stunned and stranded on the shore,
a flailing thing that strove each moment of its life,
abandoned to a beached endurance, and decay.

A dull lead light descends where radiance effused
and umbral chasms gape where full realities
once glowing in their presence met me with allure;
now something even emptier than brute survival,
a state more stolid, bland, than mere banality,
or anything that could pretend to any purpose

recedes without me in a way I cannot claim…
Here all just is – for what? My appetite erodes
to staleness and inertia, void of any care,
my ardour dims and only drains of all attachment,
ebbs and fades to darkness, ebbs and disappears,
with me the witness to the hollow time I span.

When Gods First Thundered

When gods first thundered – he or she stood up
and left the huddle of the trembling pack.
Outside the cave the lightning cleft the sky,
seared through the darkness with a snaking crack-
crack-crackling slash before the awful groan
of waking giants boomed across the earth…
A squatting shape outside, unmoved by fear
in thoughtful calm, traced glyphic zigzags in
the sand while humming low melodic moans
whose cadence coaxed the others to emerge
and gather round; and they saw purpose, form,
in what was done and softly hummed along.
The trembling cave-dogs stayed within, and by
song's end the gods allied themselves to men.

A Writer's Monologue

Let's face it, it's become a burden living
with him –
he thinks out loud, disjointedly muttering,
and forces me to listen,
but then he sinks in silence, oblivious to
my presence, and back to whatever else
he's doing;

I sense his interjections come of some unseen
and secret spasm –
an inner pressure,
where at the eruption of a sudden thought
or recollection,
his babbled sifting of syllables amounts
to a shudder.

His ponderous way is taxing, disturbing;
forever blurting
conundrums, scenarios,
and how best to state them,
he mars our peace; my wife's
been known to air annoyance and wish
he'd leave.

We can't go on like this, his butting in
each time,
sporadic mumblings drawing
attention and people looking
askance, and because of our
uncanny resemblance, imputing to me
the blame!

Abstractedly mumbling to himself, now pen
in hand,
he's struggling with
some vision of imperfect clarity;
one of us will have to leave, it seems;
returning to his page, I fear it must
be me.

Haunted

I roam the run-down manor of a mind,
it's old familiar vagueness in the dark,
it's gloomy alcoves traced with mournful eyes
and ruffled curtains roused by ghosted husks;
damp rooms where muted murmurs bruise the air,
and stale vexations tediously rehearsed,
as steps, exerted up to landless stairs,
stop short at cul-de-sacs of gaping space.
As always there, persistent mystery
implies some hidden prize or splendid gain
for which I fumble, ineffectually,
until in one grey smudge of glare, I glean
a mirrored face afloat its ageless glass –
obscure of gaze, I dare not brave with mine.

Community

After survival's fight or flight and day-long toil
and labour, sparrows in a bird bath take delight
in wallowing wings awash with wafted water;
amid the gather of a raucous splash and chatter
in sundown's savoured slow aglow and crimson linger,
some playful few adieu to jostled leaves, take off
and flit into a tree above the plashing patter;
disporting madly in a rustled bustling tussle
of laughter there like children with a cheeky twitter,
descend again and dive-bomb down the bath's bull'seye
to shrapnel lax companions with the exploded water;
some jolted from repose awoken with surprise
while others seem to see the joke and wryly chitter,
but easy all in their release, and seeming less
like mere machines within a predetermined order,
are more a free community of mirthful beings
beyond survival's freeze, or fight or flight or slaughter.

War and Society

As sure as mortal bodies ail and die –
as will this universe itself, one day –
so then the proudest empires must decline
and pale to senescence, then pass away;
for by the common law of entropy,
chaos undoes the weave of everything,
and there's no order, force or empery,
not tending to a destined scattering;
which means that wars, an unavoidable curse,
are cataclysmic blazons of oblivion,
where orders, ripe to rottenness, disperse,
while others raise another vain dominion;
but yet, we cannot live by doom's dictates
and, come what may, must still defy the Fates.

Vessel

My days are a shambles –
neglectful of friends
bestrewn like something broken,
or sieves that can't retain
a positive emotion…

My days are a shambles –
useless self-absorption
fractures like a vase
that cannot still or hold
a leaking motion…

My days lack grace
and purpose drained – or formed –
impels an urgency
for which recall now throws
the vessel that's this poem.

The Double Woman

Well, if I would be honest with myself,
I'd say I'm one half darkness, one half light,
further then, putting by defensive stealth,
I'm two parts woman in the man you sight.
And she is modest, caring, all that's bright –
beyond exaggeration, even pure,
while yet, no less a creature of the night
who'll lewdly bait me with her crude allure;
and hers the native life of innocence
for she is truly the eternal child,
yet, deadly too in her concupiscence,
she'll woo and then abandon me, reviled;
seduced, I wish this phantom no will tames
allowed our shackled lives concordant aims.

Wax Man

There was a fickle man of wax,
so delible, smooth and white,
whiter than sheets all freshly laid
and paler than a fright.

So soft was he as soft can be
and easily impressed,
whatever anyone opined
he thought agreement best;

for he was such a mellow tallow
and given to a whim
that anyone's authority
would set its seal on him;

and this took place habitually
though why could not be guessed,
but this is why – when others spoke
he'd nod assenting lest

he be imputed for a fool
and roundly dubbed a clout,
in any case to mitigate
the fear of standing out.

If men should laugh, he laughed out loud
and if they cried – he wept,
and he would strive to keep awake
till those around him slept.

If men were tender, many are,
he'd softly wax so lyrical,
but should they turn acerbic, gruff,
then he would wax satirical.

When hard men boasted of their strength
to toughness too he tend,
a puzzling strength in that it proved
his willingness to bend!

And people much adored him, yes,
they saw themselves in him,
as for himself he was a quiz
and somewhat rather dim;

for he possessed no inner core
from circumstance immune,
in changing fortune he would blanch
and quickly change his tune!

No, there was nothing he believed
he could not later falter,
his creed was good for just as long
as others did not alter.

But once he met a fateful flame
that knew him to be wax,
it got a grip he could not shake
nor force it to relax!

It smarted so, got on his wick,
and slowly laid him low,
but though he pleaded it got worse
and would not let him go!

It wanted him for who he was,
and gnawingly consumed,
and try appease it as he might
he knew that he was doomed!

For down and down it rendered him,
his body ran in tears,
and as he melted, smaller yet,
the brighter grew his fears!

And no agreeable kind of chat
could stay its appetite,
it fiercely chewed at him until
it whittled down his height;

and surely nothing, bit by bit,
would stop its ceaseless creep
until he ended as he'd lived –
a kind of formless heap.

Mythic Autumn Spectacle

On riffled leaves I walk the streets of fiction,
each step enacted through the paper smiles
and players of a universal masque;
there's little heroic in this day's display
which, yet, evokes the tragic, if banal,
as nymph-like women, Dionysian men –
alluring posers of ideal depiction –
purvey the joy of any purchased ware.
One sees how paranoiacs might descend
to abject states of absolute suspicion
as hired mimes conspire a bovine calm
with each paraded bait's inuring chant: –
beware that leering siren, brand in hand,
that surging hydra's heads – a herd of men.

Protean Look

The immensity of…
There's the sweetest guile
in your gentle love –
and oh that smile!

A perplexing turn…
There's a sharper shade
in your parted lips –
each tooth a blade!

Perpetuity hails…
Oh, that floral dress!
You – emergent Spring
with sprightly press.

In the blinking of an…
The allure that pales –
your alighting eyes
descend like flails.

Born Again

Those Saturdays of never being good
enough, whose way of thorny anguish to
the scented rosewood of the confessional
now make me wonder who I was, and laugh.
By what dark logic did a tortured heart
concede abasement drew one close to God?
'Mid all the 'good news' why was misery
the gift, and why amid the talk of sweet
compassion was it meted with a rod?
It's gone: their fear, their gloom, their sadist's hell,
the twisted hatred of the human self,
and now, at last, I thrive in my good cheer –
Redeemed from those blasphemers of this life
the sacred now has never been so near.

The Decision

Invisibly, indelibly,
an interior tear I keep
defines the rift between what is
and that which could've been.

The trace of that alternative
is always here, with me,
the place of its persistence, though,
a sealed what could've been.

I should have run without delay
when you were most in need,
the hand I held when I vowed love
is just what should've been.

But standing still, so easy then,
is hardest, now, for me,
not there with you each day I'm where
I know I should've been.

Cycles – a Rondel

It's we who think we know it all,
though ages past thought too as well;
be sure, they had as much to tell
whose worth we may account as small.

Each age's bluster must appall
as ours some ways must too repel,
it's we who think we know it all
though ages past thought too as well.

And so the highest rise to fall
the more their pride is wont to swell,
yet we like they who sadly fell
affirming hold, beyond recall –
it's we who think we know it all!

A Final Valentine

Her nature was to tend to float – float
to where the air was thin
and hard to breathe,
and she, defying gravity, unpinned,

and starved to lightness tossed as thistle-down
or gossamer strands unseen,
would rise and mount
the air, alone, and ride her grief unfound.

Once, on a mountain peak, a gaping chasm
seemed a daunting task;
atremble on all fours,
she crawled across its sheer and narrow pass.

At last, a heaviness of heart seduced
her to a nuptial rite
with partnered dread –
gave up herself, a plunging bride – to height.

Duality

Eyes captive to an imaged vitality
behold the morning's open portal for
their fare, its sanguine sheen, and rosy blush,
its radiant petals spun of spectral flesh;
imbibing floral liquor, a lustrous gaze
laps up the lucent cup whose nectar spurs
a mystery whose savour never sates…
Black vault beyond the dawn's diurnal roll,
I kneel before your second way's abyss,
and paying tribute to these dusky depths
surrender to the sweep and nether shades
of burning thirst's illimitable clefts;
in dual-you – my joy's enigma, goal
and sauce, I drain a dun and russet end.

Pinning

It is a dead, dread thing,
a fatal hand,
that pins a butterfly
awaft in spring
and keeps it like a flake
of snow beneath
a glass of perpetual winter.

Lullaby

If you suffer a horrid insomnia,
a painful, fatiguing alertness,
and, prostrate like one with a hernia,
just long for a blissful inertness,

there's many a drastic expedient
which you have most likely not tried,
yes, many a calming ingredient,
but let's set aside suicide.

Instead, I suggest you might ponder
this rustic but safe remedy,
'Unlikely,' you'll think, but no wonder,
when *did* you last read poetry?

I tell you just pull out some verses,
the good stuff malignly called doggerel,
for consciousness nothing disperses
than the very best verse of McGonagall.

Now, perhaps you've attempted valerian
but cursed its effects didn't take,
those classics I say, Spenserian,
were made so you can't keep awake.

Or has it been fennel or hops,
or something like neat aniseed?
Forget 'em, all useless ol' crops,
Pope's just the narcotic you need!

You might've tried honey and milk,
but better, no doubt, and terrific
the very name Pound and that ilk
betoken straight off, 'soporific'!

You might've tried tinctures expensive
or tippled until you're a-tottle
or done it like Thomas, intensive,
and knocked off the whole bloody bottle,

but that's self-destructive, untenable,
a serious abuse of medicine,
a healthier way, amenable,
is just to flick through some Tennyson.

Avoid entertainers like Lear
he'll keep you awake, not a doubt,
but stick to your Milton and Shakespeare,
by common accord a knockout!

Besides, don't forget the romantics,
who blather so sonorously,
or those of confessional antics
who suffer monotonously.

I tell you, you'll cease in being restive
if you take up those scratchers of quills
and if my advice ineffective
then turn to your tablets and pills.

For who but those poets profound
could fashion with taxing preponderance
a moment as if it hung round
with heavy perpetual somnolence?

Of course, there are poets contemporary
as tiresome as any of these,
but look on my few as exemplary –
I've tallied enough enemies!

The watchdogs of culture, like pugs,
will bristle and howl – 'barbarian',
poor addicts inured to the drugs
they sneak from their bardic herbarium;

and so, I will suffer their scorn
for being a barbarous creep,
methinks though I heareth thee yawn,
oops no, that's a snore – you're asleep!

Pettiness and the Big News

Time after time, it happens,
the surface all seems calm
but yet you brood
and hold as precious –
imagined or real – a slight;

with petty hurt and malice,
you nurse your wound, a weapon,
with which to scorn
the imaged friend
you feel had let you down.

And when he culpably looms
in nowhere but your mind,
then wield the wound
just like a knife
to cut him down to size.

So wield it there forever,
your triumph every time;
but then there comes
the awful news –
yesterday he died.

Barren Road

Here now the day of sudden warning
where ill at ease of self prevails,
the overdue undo now dawning
along too long's neglectful trail.

This now the time of breathless choking
upon perhaps' no return,
down through the way of no revoking
what wise regret cannot unlearn.

The sign, 'amends', hangs cracked and broken,
grimed by the traffic's ceaseless surge,
its witness, man, now long the token
of some incredulous, senseless urge,

moves on inertial to an end
that opens like a waiting void,
uncertain how each step to bend
to that, his home, each step destroyed.

Little Green Transgressors

We'll never comprehend your fictive orders,
your artificial zones of ownership;
you mix the real up with imagined borders
between whose cracks we unavoidably slip.
We weave inexorably between your fences,
find niches in your world of concrete clutter;
and though you root us out for these offences
we rise again, undaunted, from the gutter!
We don't pretend to be the world's possessors,
and make no claim on what exists for all,
ours is a modest way, we meek transgressors,
discreetly working round restrictive walls…
Heed us, life's dogged champions everywhere
by whom you pass most often, unaware.

Fishbowl

Each day – through a labyrinth of cameras –
I feel myself grow fins…
With every inconspicuous lure
and hook, a body of scales
deforms my former skin.

Through every site I surf –
in my case swim –
the calls or emails traced
like droppings in my wake –
my lungs morph into gills.

Plopped in this binary realm –
a fish in some
colossal cyber tank's
assiduously filtered medium –
I leave observable loops

or lines from pane to pane
or float here fixed
in the intrusive glare…
For whose delight or fishy interest
am I an ornament?

Before whose hidden eye
do I parade?
By what collector's urge
or merchant's hand
am I here captured in this net,

exposed and flailing – breathless –
my gasping efforts
held before another's
secret gaze
and inscrutable intent?

Lovebird

Love is a bird who is hungry for justice,
hobbling abjectly and sobbing her song,
sorely desirous of human affection, or
even the merest attentative crumb.

Waiting, forsaken, at revelry's table,
eyeing those feasting with famished fatigue,
Love is expiring in midst of the fanfare of
fatuous excess and stupefied greed.

Mind Drift

I

Lace-sifted flits the languid light;
sun-winnowed, swayed in flecks
of faint autumnal gold,
it laps a sleepy soaked
and dream-dropped eye;

so weightlessly across
a face transported, skips
and drifts a liquid glide,
a dance of dappled wafts
and breezy daubs.

In timeless ease until
a selfless surface broke,
a bleary I afloat
so gropes against the tide
of dazzling light.

In a weary-wake and eddy, rise
and bob in time, then melt
and fall and drown, weave in
and out the liquid body
in recline.

Amid the first unfathomed wastes,
a drunken head the captain,
embark on helmless leagues
and dawning in a dream,
dream woken time.

II

Curtain of lace and grime,
gauze-filtered light
soft rippling through
its heaving folds,
light laving on
my dreaming face
as if reflecting from
a limpid pool,
that's how, half-wakeful,
I come to this
wet driftwood dream
flesh bound in water;
that's how I steep
in running light,
that's how I wake
to find a bleary I
and partly woke
and still
sub-
    merging time…

That's how…
I must remember,
I must interpret,
I must know this,
know this…
Not now…

III

Over the rooftops I incline,
past terracotta reds and browns
encrusted pale in lichen green,
and then descend, so smoothly down,
and skim along the concrete paths;

pale rain-sheen road aglitter in
the sun, returns my bob and rise,
each echo of my walking waves
reflected in my moving eyes
as they serrate suburban wastes.

Under the rain-dashed trees, the leaf-
blades blazing in autumnal light,
the scented atmospheres of damp
and mould infuse a green-tinged mood
of still lagoons and algae ponds.

As iridescent green as starling breasts,
electric as that glistening slime
which smears the red-brick wall I pass,
as moist, as green and fresh as time's
this flotsam mood a mind sails through.

Out, out into the open light
and past the paint-stripped picket fence,
beyond the brilliant iron gate
emblazoned with its streaks of rust,
and down the cobbled lane of broken glass.

'But where this winding drift, where to?'
'To factories on a norward bearing…'
And then a thought, a crucial one,
but lost. Some overwhelming thought
forgotten by a driftwood mind

on a wayward-wending journey…

IV

Distantly looming into view,
hulking and monumental,
a blue-asbestos-roof horizon
and corrugated ring of metal

ascends the known world's rim.
Onward on tides of leaves and butts,
a sea mosaic of cracked gum pods,
of flasks with logos peeling off;

onward over strips of grass,
discarded packs of cigarettes,
beer cans and bottles, paper barks,
wrappers and fast-food scraps;

past trash a dog serenely snouts,
along a rusty cyclone fence,
the wrecker's yard of twangs
and tangles, burrs and barbs,

its monstrous snags the tentacles
that draw sleep's seamen to
unwary deaths, and where
near whirling wind-torn melodies

and whorls of enormous seaweed wire,
a dream-mate cries, 'Beware that song!
Off starboard sings a siren choir,
beware that deadly song, and ho!

Those breakers yonder – ho!'
The panel-beater's hammer falls
with thunderous white and squalling roars,
and slouching up its glinting form

the foundry lifts its molten maw…
'No breakers there!' that dream-mate cries,
'But some sea-dragon's rolling form,
those stacks the blowholes spewing foam!

There, risen in a snorted plume,
smell acrid fumes of oil and coal,
a raging slick where some good ship
falls prey and founders, smashed and torn…'

'To port side hard – fast tack about,
before the wind and bear her south,
these latitudes of a dreaming mind
have drawn us off our charted course…

Hold south, me mates, I now recall
that thought I thought I'd long forgot!
In hand I bear here me commission,
in hand is me consignment note!

Two days from here we'll have her stowed
with all the cargo she can hold,
look here, me map and shopping list:
three onions, tomatoes, flour and milk,

two lemons, thyme, and four lamb chops,
deodorant, baguettes, potatoes, oil,
some plastic wrap, black pepper, salt,
a roll of aluminium foil,

some vinegar, garlic, turnips, swedes,
and blades to trim these matted beards,
a pack of rice and margarine,
sardines and nutmeg, one baked beans,

oh yes, corned beef, a tin of peas,
some swabs for me infected ear;
hold faith, hold hope me haggard men,
for most of all, there's rum and beer!'

A cataract of howls ascends,
a waterspout of withheld joy,
all hands bend backs in earnest toil
to El Dorados of alcohol...

V

There is a moment where a mind becalmed,
lulled softly by the plash of ceaseless waves,
dissolves amid immensities of silence
and trembles to the feeblest stir of sound.
Then, suddenly, a plover's scratchy cry,
hurled hard against that bowl of blue, assaults
the startled ear as if it scuffed the sky.
Then, huddled with itself, a seaman's gaze
wrung back from deep unconscious voids,
made palpable again with fear, pursues
that bird above the abject wastes and casts
a vertiginous eye beyond its line
of vanished flight to seize where it might land…

'In emptiness, immense, that bird might land,
in boundless space, beyond, a gaze might rest,'
a chap-lipped mouth repeats beneath its breath…

Sound falls, one hardly knows one speaks at all…

But soon the weary mind dissolves again,
and soon, subdued, once more contained within
that vast enfolding hush… And this the hour
of dreadful calm where you are melded with
the depths you never know you are; and this
the hour of luckless happening and hazard
where voices sing in you as from afar…

VI

This is the song that ruins men,
too sweet and dainty to resist,
a siren song for which they long,
and promises eternal rest.

'In us,' they sing, 'in us who are
reflections of all you desire,
fulfilment is a boundless spring
in which all care can quench its fire.

Ah, bring your parched and thirsty lips
and drink to fullness of our kisses,
lay languid heads upon our laps
and slumber to our glib caresses.

Oh come, enfolded in our arms,
and fall, let fall your will to us,
lap swollen breasts of foaming milk
and let all worthless sorrows pass.

Now plunge your face in scented hair,
fold in our turbid rolling curves,
ah, lose yourself in our soft depths
and lie with us in deep-sea caves…'

VII

There is a moment where a mind becalmed
remembers something of itself in stillness,
and understands the wheeling arc of sea
and sky revolves with deadly apparitions.
Unmoved by visions born of its delirium,
the thirsting soul recalls itself as source
of succour and affliction, gathers itself
once more and finds an inner poise and wisdom…

(How mournful seems the dying sun as he
descends into the western chamber of
the sea, his downcast brow and dimming eye
forlornly facing imminent defeat,
his golden locks now sparely spread, an old
man's head of hair – oh may he rise again!)

Let sirens sing their lays for I'll not follow
into the hollows where delirious sailors meet
foul ends, there picked of flesh and strewn of bone.
Their silky song already turns to curses hoarse,
their eyes now flicker with a lurid glow,
their once immaculate faces, splendid, soft,
contort with skull-like malice and derision.
This is disaster's song of death, not love!
This is the dirge of tombstones, and not life!
The wind is up, unleashed from deep within
my heart, as if approaching from afar!

'All hands on deck and ring the muster bell!
Blot out that song those sirens spew, it is
the fractured patchwork of a fraying mind.'
A-ring-a-ding-ding! 'Dream-mates seal your ears
with wax and stop that deadly song they sing.'

'Why flee from us who are your joy
and promise of unbounded pleasure,
we riches of the deep sea's store
and more than mortal mind can measure?

Why shun the chance of endless bliss,
to waste and die upon the flux?
Oh, would you have perpetual life?
Then come, draw nearer to these rocks!

Oh fools! Sad fools! You are not men
who run like mice from ones so fair!
Poor cowards, where those bravest hearts
that win the world if but they dare?

What mortal woman could bestow
a share of her eternity?
But come to us, return, and we'll
confer you immortality!

A curse on you, you weakling men,
you shrunken boys and timid fools,
we pray our Sire Poseidon may
engulf you to a coward's doom…'

A-ring-a-ding-ding…
'Land ahoy, to port
side Captain foam the heads of ale, at ten
o'clock, ahoy! And there, beyond the heads,
and frothing peaks of glorious amber, there
at last, in rum-red haze, the bottle-shop!
A-ring-a-ding-ding
a-ring-a-ding-ding
a-ring-a-ding-ding…

VIII

'Turn off that thing!' my tired wife frowns.

A-ring-a ding-ding
a-ring-a-ding-ding…

Hard grains of sleep encrusting my eye,
bright light still pooling on my face,
I fumble for the switch.
A-ring-a ding –

'It's ten o'clock, we're late,
should've done the shopping yesterday,'
she mutters with a squinting eye.
'Make us a cuppa love.'

Her voice sinks softly within herself…

Beside me in her nude
perfection, I pause, watch her lie.
A twisted sheet about her hips,
her hair drawn over her weary face,
she looks as if she's been tossed up
on some far shore or mythic beach…

Uncannily, the sheet about her folds
as if it were a foamy wave,
or water ebbing from a reef,
from which a white-transparent arm
and torso float, then flutter to
the vagrant eddies of the sea;
more so, as filtered curtain light
across her neck and shoulder
streams like a spumy filigree.

How like strange seaweed seems
that tangled hair across her face,
how like the distant call and hiss
of breakers hums her gentle breath…

But ah, that face, so heavy in
mortality, engraved and lined in time;
how so unlike a siren's in
its open honesty,
and just itself, untouched
by the desiring of
a dreaming mind…

How warm in its transparency,
how palpably real
and patient in endurance,
how worthy of my belief
in she who trusts
belief in me!

How worthy of love…

Those sirens sweet, for all
their wild seductive beauty
and unsurpassable grandeur,
will never know this pure solidity
and steadfastness,
they'll never know
the yielded fragility
of a lover's face here given
even while it here recedes!

Unlike the feeble trumpery
of protean charms
reflecting back their wanton lies,
her face, so gathered in
her sleep's humility,
encompassed in its own
untouchable hush,
withdraws in its mortality
and yet is here, continues here,
and gives itself to me.

'I'm still waiting for that cuppa, love,'
she mutters beneath her breath.
'And so you are, my love.'
I kiss her naked shoulder, rise,
then stumble to the kitchen in
the dying vestige of a dream,
the faintest hint of sea salt on my lips.

House Builder

As with the birth of love comes joy apace
and in that joy contentment held secure,
it is of love I'd build a dwelling place
to keep us joyous in its warm allure;
and it would humbly stand of common clay,
variant stones through whose asymmetry,
contending faces formed an interplay
of something that defies disparity;
for set harmoniously of modest earth
and differing dividuals, deftly blent,
it would of hurdles men erect to mirth
confound impossibility's dissent.
But why rebuild what is and was, will be?
This house is here – in actuality.

www.ingramcontent.com/pod-product-compliance
Lightning Source LLC
Chambersburg PA
CBHW070335120526
44590CB00017B/2896